Horatio Rogers

Discourse before the Rhode Island Historical Society

At its Centennial Celebration of Rhode Island's Adoption of the Federal

Constitution

Horatio Rogers

Discourse before the Rhode Island Historical Society
At its Centennial Celebration of Rhode Island's Adoption of the Federal Constitution

ISBN/EAN: 9783744735094

Printed in Europe, USA, Canada, Australia, Japan

Cover: Foto ©ninafisch / pixelio.de

More available books at **www.hansebooks.com**

DISCOURSE

BEFORE THE

Rhode Island Historical Society

AT ITS CENTENNIAL CELEBRATION OF

RHODE ISLAND'S ADOPTION

OF THE

FEDERAL CONSTITUTION,

IN PROVIDENCE, R. I., MAY 29, 1890,

BY

HORATIO ROGERS,

PRESIDENT OF THE SOCIETY;

TOGETHER WITH OTHER PROCEEDINGS ON
THAT OCCASION.

PUBLISHED BY THE SOCIETY.

The Providence Press:
SNOW & FARNHAM, PRINTERS.
37 Custom House Street.
1890.

At the Quarterly Meeting of the Rhode Island Historical Society, held July 1, 1890, the thanks of the Society were tendered to the President of Brown University for the use of Sayles Memorial Hall; to Professor B. W. Hood and the High School Choir for their fine music: to the Orator for his eloquent and scholarly discourse; and to all other participants in the Centennial Celebration, by the Society, of Rhode Island's Adoption of the Federal Constitution, for their able and satisfactory services; and it was voted that one thousand copies of the discourse and the other proceedings be printed for the use of the Society.

CENTENNIAL CELEBRATION

OF

RHODE ISLAND'S ADOPTION

OF THE

FEDERAL CONSTITUTION.

AT the Quarterly Meeting of the Rhode Island Historical Society held April 2, 1889, Messrs. William D. Ely and John A. Howland and Rev. W. F. B. Jackson were appointed a committee to make arrangements for a suitable celebration by the Society of Rhode Island's Adoption of the Federal Constitution, May 29, 1890. Upon the death of Mr. Howland, the Rev. Dr. E. Benjamin Andrews was appointed to fill the vacancy, and the committee subsequently reported the following order of commemorative proceedings to be holden in Sayles Memorial Hall, at 7½ o'clock P. M.

The Hon. George M. Carpenter, First Vice-President of the Society, and United States District Judge for the District of Rhode Island, to preside.

Singing of patriotic songs by a choir of pupils from the Providence High School, under the direction of Professor B. W. Hood.

Prayer by the Rev. Dr. E. Benjamin Andrews, Second Vice-President of the Society, and President of Brown University.

Discourse by General Horatio Rogers, President of the Society.

Benediction by the Rev. Dr. Andrews.

"America," by the choir.

At the time and place appointed "there was," in the words of the *Providence Journal,* "a large and notable gathering," and the prescribed programme was successfully carried out. A half-hour of song by the choir was succeeded by the following

PRAYER BY THE REV. DR. E. BENJAMIN ANDREWS.

Eternal Spirit, the Creator of Man and the Ordainer of History, we would reverently recognize Thee as we meet this evening to set up a memorial pillar upon the great highway of time. We thank Thee for the marvellous career of the Commonwealth in which we dwell. We believe it to have been of Thy divine counsel and goodness that here upon these beautiful shores, from the first, and earlier than at any other spot upon our planet, men were permitted to worship God according to the dictates of their own consciences ; and that the lively experiment was here put forth in faith of erecting a constitution of government to have validity only in civil things. Almighty God, it is because this tree of religious liberty was planted by Thy own right hand that it did not wither and die, but rather sent out noble branches graciously to beshadow all the States of our beloved land : yea, and even yielded fruit for the life of the other nations of the earth. Forgive us, O Righteous Judge, if some pride should mingle with our thanksgiving, as we reflect that the one clear and unchallenged contribution which America has made to the civilization of mankind has proceeded from the favored community to which we belong.

O God, our fathers were not always wise. They could not on all occasions see the right way or read the signs of their times. They could not perfectly make out the future. May we, and may all men, judge them with circumspection and with charity. They were conscientious; and we bless Thee that Thou didst lead them better than they knew, at last to cast in their lot with the great sisterhood of States in company with whom they had fought out their liberties.

Bestow abundance of Thy Spirit upon Thy servant who shall at this time array before our thoughts the events of that critical period ; so that from his words all present may take deeper reverence for the past and firmer hope regarding the future. May we learn to trust in principles, even when they are new and unpopular ; knowing that as the world is ruled by the God of truth, they who are of the truth and of the light shall assuredly triumph in the end. Bless the Nation of which, happily, we now form part. Bless our State. Be with its civil officers from highest to lowest, and with all its people. May righteousness, public spirit, and lofty ideas and ideals so prevail among us that when in another hundred years men gather, as we now gather, to review the past, we may not seem altogether unworthy to be thought of along with the mighty departed whom we delight to honor. Amen!

The Hon. George M. Carpenter, who presided, introduced the Orator of the occasion in these words :

LADIES AND GENTLEMEN : It is to commemorate the accession of the State of Rhode Island to the National Government that we have invited your presence this evening, — an event of the greatest import to our own people, and not without consequence to the Nation.   I say, advisedly, the accession of our State ; because the adoption of the Constitution by our State was not only later in point of time but different in character from the action of most of the original States. We joined ourselves to a Nation already established and in the full exercise of governmental power, and in so doing we yielded our existence as an independent and sovereign State. Fully appreciating the character and the consequences of this action, we chose a time later than that which seemed convenient to other States. Having made ourselves part of the new Nation, we may say, without pre-sumption, that we have not failed in our allegiance and that we have not been wanting to the Nation in council or in the field of battle.   But we think it becoming that, on this anniversary, and under the direction of this Society, there should be made a definitive and authoritative statement of the reasons which impelled us first to hesitate with anxious deliberation, and afterwards freely and fully to abandon our independent character and become an integral part of an indissoluble Nation.   This declaration should be made in such form that it shall be the end of controversy, and that the future student of history may require no further material for a just and discriminating conclusion.   For the delivery of such a statement I now have the honor to present the President of the Society, General Horatio Rogers.

GENERAL ROGERS'S DISCOURSE.

Mr. President, Ladies and Gentlemen : We have met to celebrate a great event in the history of Rhode Island. On this centennial anniversary of her adoption of the federal constitution I shall endeavor to trace the causes of her delay in ratifying that instrument, for she was the last of the original thirteen states to avail herself of its provisions, and she has been bitterly assailed for not more speedily parting with that independent sovereignty which some of her more rapid sister states have since spent four years in bloody warfare in seeking to regain.

Rhode Island, to borrow the language of her General Assembly, in 1845, when resenting the interference of the Legislature of Maine in matters growing out of the Dorr War, so called, "can never . . . forget her past history—her early struggles in the cause of religious freedom—her toils, and sufferings, and sacrifices, in the War of the Revolution, and her jealous determination, at all times, to secure to the people of Rhode Island the exclusive right to manage their own affairs in their own way." [1]

These words of her official representatives afford the key to Rhode Island's action on more than one occasion, and, broadly speaking, furnish the explanation of her conduct in regard to the federal constitution.

[1] Proceedings in the Rhode Island Legislature on Sundry Resolutions of the State of Maine, 5; also R. I. Acts and Resolves, June Session, 1845, p. 49.

Our first settlers were, in a double sense, the children of oppression, "wee beinge an outcast people," they wrote, when addressing Richard Cromwell, the Lord Protector, in 1659, "formerly from our mother nations in the Bishops' daies, and since from the rest of the new English over zealous collonys."[1] Roger Williams and the other founders of Providence, the Antinomians who settled at Newport, Samuel Gorton, of Warwick, and still later the Quakers, were all thrust out of Massachusetts-Bay for conscience sake.

The hand of oppression reached them even in exile. The United Colonies of New England, which, in 1643, formed a league for mutual protection, absolutely refused to admit Rhode Island to their fellowship.[2] When the charter of 1643-4 was granted to this colony the same old persecuting spirit of her neighbors prevented for three years an organization under it. Governor Winthrop, of Massachusetts-Bay, in his History of New England,[3] tells us that Plymouth sent one of her magistrates to Aquidneck Island to forbid the exercise of any pretended authority there, claiming it to be under her jurisdiction. "Our court," he continues, "also sent to forbid them to exercise any authority within that part of our jurisdiction at Pawtuxent and Mishaomet ; and although they had boasted to do great matters there by virtue of their charter, yet they dared not to attempt anything." Connecticut claimed jurisdiction over Rhode Island territory west of Narragansett Bay, and Massachusetts over that east of it, and not until 1726[4] was the former obliged by the decision

[1] 1 R. I. Col. Records, 414.
[2] 2 Hazard's State Papers, 2°, 96.
    Ed. of 1853, vol. 2, 270.
[4] The order of the King in Council was passed February 8, 1726; 4 R. I. Col. Rec., 370.
The boundary line was not run by commissioners appointed by the two colonies until 1728 :
; R. I. Col. Rec., 400, 411, and 413.

of the King in Council to withdraw her assumption; and it was 1746[1] before the latter, likewise, was compelled to yield up her usurpation, when the territory embraced within the towns of Tiverton, Little Compton, Bristol, Warren, Barrington and Cumberland, passed from the jurisdiction of Massachusetts to that of Rhode Island.

Notwithstanding the hands of her neighbors were against her, the little colony survived and sustained herself. When our founders ascertained that they could not preserve their liberties within the limits of Massachusetts-Bay, bitter experience taught them they could do so beyond her borders. When the United Colonies refused to receive the outcast colony into their confidence and under their protection, she found she could exist without their aid and notwithstanding their opposition. These early experiences, and the isolating effects of her steadfast adherence to the principle and practice of soul-liberty, despite all pressure brought to bear upon her, developed in Rhode Island, beyond all the other original American colonies, a self-reliance, a force of character, and an independence of feeling and action, that enabled her to successfully resist influences that would have absorbed or overthrown a less sturdy colony.

At one period Rhode Island was the most radical, and at another, the most conservative, of all the old thirteen colonies or states. At a bound she leaped far in advance of them all in her cardinal principle of soul-liberty. Every one worshiped God as he pleased. Baptist, Quaker and Antinomian, Jew and Gentile, the observer of the first day of the week, and

---

[1] The order of the King in Council was passed May 28, 1746. The Rhode Island Commissioners appointed to run the eastern boundary line in accordance with the Royal determination, reported to the General Assembly at its January session, 1746-7 : 5 R. I. Col. Rec. 197 and 199.

the observer of the seventh day, and members of all other
creeds, here found a safe harbor of refuge. The law called
on no one to contribute to the support of a minister of
religion ; and herein, for more than a century and a half, the
little colony was utterly out of touch and sympathy with her
neighbors, for in Massachusetts and Connecticut, strange as
it may seem, not until after the advent of the present century were church and state entirely divorced. The colonial
charter of Rhode Island, likewise, was unsurpassed in liberality. That of Connecticut alone approached it, and in
these two colonies only, until after independence, were the
governors elected by the people. So liberal were the royal
charters of these two colonies that they alone survived the
Revolution, Connecticut abandoning her charter in 1818, and
Rhode Island clinging to hers until 1842. The people of
Rhode Island and their representatives have always exerted
a stronger direct influence on governmental affairs, and still
exert it, than in any other colony or state ; and nowhere was
or still is there a greater jealousy of official or other centralized power. Until within a few years the people directly, or
through their representatives in General Assembly, elected
nearly all their officers, and only recently has the Governor,
to any considerable extent, been invested with an appoint-
ing power. He never had the veto power, and in many other
respects his authority is much more circumscribed than in
other states. This jealousy of centralized power that has
always existed in colony and state has in some degree survived to our day, and is well illustrated in our present constitution. Each town and city has one senator in the upper
branch of the General Assembly, and there, Jamestown
with less than a thousand inhabitants, is the peer of the city
of Providence with more than 130,000. In the lower house

each town has at least one representative, and no town or city can have more than twelve, or one-sixth of the whole, the body being limited to seventy-two members; and yet Providence contains nearly two-fifths of the whole population of the state. [1] No act of incorporation, other than for religious, literary, and charitable purposes, or for a military or fire company, can be passed by the General Assembly to whom it is first presented, but must be continued over another election of members, so that the will of the people may have an opportunity to be expressed upon it. In no other state, until eighteen months ago, was the elective franchise so restricted. Nowhere has town government been so rigidly adhered to. Even in Connecticut, state senators are now elected from districts regardless of town lines; and in Massachusetts, county officers have charge of probate matters and the recording of deeds. Nowhere on the face of the earth to-day, Great Britain and her colonies not excepted, do the old English common law forms of procedure and practice prevail to such an extent as in the courts of Rhode Island. The very liberality of her cardinal principle and of her royal charter seems to have made her fearful of losing what of liberty she

---

[1] Prior to the constitution of 1842, ten assistants were annually elected, who, together with the governor, or, in his absence or by his permission, the deputy-governor, constituted the upper house of the General Assembly. The composition of the lower house, until the constitution of 1842 went into operation, afforded a most notable illustration of Rhode Island conservatism, for by King Charles's charter it was provided that Newport should have six representatives, Providence, Portsmouth and Warwick, four representatives each, and every other town and city two representatives each. However fair this may have been in 1663, when the charter was granted, it became utterly disproportionate in less than half a century thereafter, as the census of 1708 shows that Providence then had more than twice as many inhabitants as Portsmouth, and more than thrice as many as Warwick. In 1800 Providence had more inhabitants than Newport, more than three times as many as Warwick, more than four times as many as Portsmouth, and more than fifteen times as many as Jamestown; and as time went on, the disproportion grew greater and greater, but no change was made in the number of representatives till 1842.

had gained ; so the radicalism of her early days has reacted
upon her, producing an intense conservatism.

With such conservatism, and with such jealousy of centralized power, let us turn our eyes to the period of the Revolution and see how it manifested itself. Early in May,
1776,[1] the General Assembly withdrew its allegiance from
the King of Great Britain and enacted that all writs and
processes in law should thereafter issue in the name and
under the authority of "the Governor and Company
of the English Colony of Rhode Island and Providence
Plantations," to which authority alone public officers were to
swear fealty. Rhode Island having thus become an independent colony, her members of congress, elected at that same
May session, found in their commissions that year an
injunction which showed plainly how jealously independence,
even of her sister colonies, was to be guarded ; for the com-
mission after authorizing them to consult and advise upon
measures for the public weal and, in conjunction with the
delegates from the other colonies, to enter into and adopt
such measures, contained this significant provision, viz. :
"[2]taking the greatest care to secure to this colony, in the
strongest and most perfect manner, its present established
form, and all the powers of government so far as relates to
its internal police and conduct of our own affairs, civil and
religious." This provision contained the political creed of
the state ; and the real underlying cause of Rhode Island's
tardiness in accepting so radical a change as the concession
required by the federal constitution called upon her to make,
was her jealousy of centralized power and the vein of intense
conservatism that has run through her later character, mani-
festing itself so conspicuously by her tenaciously clinging,

until less than half a century ago, to the old colonial charter
with its greatly restricted suffrage ; to primogeniture—for the
eldest son was allowed to vote in preference to other sons ;
to semi-annual elections of representatives in the General Assembly ; and to many other antiquated methods ;
paper money upon which some have laid so much stress being
merely an incident and not a cause. This jealousy of centralized power and this conservatism, it will be observed,
manifested itself chiefly in the country and not in large
towns ; exactly in the localities where the same traits of
character have most manifested themselves on other occasions. With her bitter experience, Rhode Island was dis-
trustful of her neighbors. But forty years before, had she
succeeded in recovering jurisdiction over several towns, after
having been unjustly deprived of it for more than a century.
For one hundred and fifty years she had enjoyed utter eman-
cipation in religious affairs, but the neighbors that bounded
her by land on every side, were still requiring their inhabitants to contribute to the support of religious ministers for
whom many of them cared nothing. When Rhode Island
was called to merge herself with a dozen other states, of
which she was the least, and from her diminutive territory
must, perforce, ever remain so ; when she remembered that
from her nearest neighbors she had suffered much, and that
with them, in some respects, she was still not in accord ; when
she reflected that *after* she had made the concession she could
never recall it, and that this new and untried bond of union
might prove a fetter upon that freedom she had braved so
much to secure,—perhaps it is not to be wondered at that she
should have been slow to decide.

Detractors have sometimes ascribed Rhode Island's pro-
crastination in adopting the federal constitution to a gen-

eral low plane of patriotism pervading her character. Her
record during the memorable struggle for independence from
Great Britain proves that such an assumption is utterly without foundation. Rhode Island has always been intensely
patriotic. "[1]This State," wrote William Bradford, Speaker
of the Rhode Island House of Representatives, to the President of Congress, in November, 1782, " may be justly ranked
among the foremost in the common cause, having furnished
in support of it as many men and as much money, in proportion to its abilities, as any state in the Union, and much
more than most of them, and it is still disposed to continue
its exertions."

In 1783, the Continental Loan Office accounts show that
only four states had contributed more to the public treasury
than Rhode Island, diminutive as she was, and in proportion
to population none could compare with her. With less than
a quarter of the inhabitants of Maryland she held half again
as much of the public debt. Though only one-eighth as
populous as Virginia she was a public creditor in more than
double the amount of that great state; and while North
Carolina and South Carolina each possessed more than three
times the number of inhabitants of Rhode Island, yet this
state held upwards of six times more of the public debt than
the former, and upwards of seven times more than the
latter.[2]

[1] Staples's Rhode Island in the Continental Congress, 400.

[2] Madison Papers, Gilpin's Ed., 304, 431: 1 Bancroft's History of the Constitution of
the United States, 81.

If for any reason exception be taken to the Loan Office accounts as a basis of compari-
son, then it may be stated that, according to the report of the Board of Commissioners
appointed by Congress to settle the accounts of the respective states for expenses incurred
during the Revolutionary War, of the seven states to whom the United States owed bal-
ances on the last day of 1789, to which the accounts were made up, those of but three states
were larger than that of Rhode Island; while six states were largely indebted to the
United States. 2 Pitkin's Political and Civil History of the United States, 316, 538.

But it has been urged that the delegates from Rhode Island were very delinquent, at the last, in attending the Continental Congress. This was rather the fault of the members than of the state, for the delegates were duly elected, and if they neglected their duties, they but followed the example of members from other states. William Ellery, one of our delegates in Congress, in a letter to Governor Greene, dated February 1, 1784, relating to the ratification of the treaty of peace with Great Britain,[1] said :—" For the want of nine states we have not been able to transact business of importance. After having wrote many pressing letters, and sent off two expresses, nine states were at length collected, and the definitive treaty ratified. As soon as this was done, one of the Delaware members left Congress ; and there have been only eight states represented since his departure. Georgia has not had a delegate on the floor for a twelve month. New Hampshire has had but one ever since I have attended. New York is not at present represented, and New Jersey has but one member."

To the multiplicity of causes for Rhode Island's delay in adopting the federal constitution, no one, perhaps, made a larger contribution than David Howell, and yet, paradoxical as it may seem, he was in favor of it. He was a native of New Jersey and a graduate of Princeton. Removing to this state soon after graduation, he was first a tutor and then a professor in Rhode Island College. He studied law and became famous for his wit, learning and eloquence. For three years he was a member of Congress, and in 1786 he was one of the judges of the court in the great case of Trevett vs. Weeden, that adjudged some of the extravagant paper money legislation of that year unconstitutional. Subsequently he

[1] Staples, 468.

was at different times Attorney-General of the State, United
States District Attorney, and for the last fourteen years of
his life United States District Judge. From 1790 to 1824 he
held the chair of law in Brown University. He was a member of Congress from 1782 to 1785, and there, it was, that his
unflinching advocacy of state rights, often contending single-
handed against the whole house, roused bitter opposition
both to him and to his state. Strong and pronounced in his
views, he was fearless and outspoken in maintaining them.
Policy and conciliation formed no part of his character. He
was uncompromisingly opposed to granting to the Confederation the right to lay a duty on imports. The system then in
force of calling upon the states for requisitions of money had
proved a miserable failure. Through lack of funds to carry
on the government the utter dissolution of the Confederation
seemed imminent. On the third day of February, 1781, Congress had recommended to the states to grant it the power to
lay an impost of five per cent., and by the articles of confederation each state must agree to its adoption. All but Georgia
and Rhode Island granted the power; the former never acted
on the recommendation, but the latter utterly refused to sanc-
tion it. Appeals were dispatched from Congress to this state,
and finally a committee was raised to come in person, but at
this juncture the great state of Virginia repealed her assent,
so the mission was abandoned, for while a little state, like
Rhode Island, could, perhaps, have been forced to yield to
pressure, no one dreamed of attempting it with a great state
like Virginia. The impost question continued a bone of
contention until the adoption of the constitution. So bitter
was the feeling in Congress against Howell for his part in
the matter, that attempts were made to break down his character and reputation and to drive him from that body. At

one time a vote of censure was sought to be passed because
of a letter he had written ; at another an effort to unseat him
was made ; but though these attempts proved futile, yet a
prejudice was excited in some quarters which was never erad-
icated.[1] A few extracts from his letters will illustrate the
tenacity of his purpose, the intensity of his utterances, the
success of his efforts, and the bitter opposition and personal
hostility he awakened. "[2] I cannot find words strong
enough," he says, " to express my indignation at the base
means, the intrigue, the chicanery, the deceit, the circumven-
tion, the fetches, the side winds, the bye blows, the am-
bushes, the stratagems, the manœuvring, the desultory attacks,
the regular approaches, the canting and snivelling, as well as
swearing and lying, and, in short, the total prostitution of
every power and faculty of body and mind and office, to
carry a point, which I need not name." Again he writes :
"[3] The states are now generally astonished that they should
ever have been led into such an error as to give Congress
the vast and uncontrollable powers contained in this ordinance.
Virginia, South Carolina and North Carolina repealed their
hasty grants, as did the lower house of Massachusetts.
Georgia and Rhode Island never granted the request of Congress." The intense hostility Mr. Howell roused by his
course is portrayed in this final extract from his correspondence. "[4] I have been in hot water," he writes, "for six or
seven weeks,—ever since business has been taken up in ear-
nest. Thank God, we have hitherto carried every point. I
have received two written challenges to fight duels : one
from Col. Mercer, of Virginia, the other from Col. Spaight, of

---

[1] Writings of William G. Goddard, Vol. I, 160, note : Howell's Correspondence in
Staples.

[2] Staples, 180.   [3] Staples, 487.   [4] Staples, 514.

2

North Carolina. The Journals will give their political char-
acters. I answered them that I meant to chastise any insult
I might receive, and laid their letters before Congress."
That I may be sure not to overstate the influence exerted by
Mr. Howell at this important period, I shall borrow a few
sentences from Chief Justice Staples, and thus fortify my-
self with the authority of his profound knowledge of Rhode
Island affairs. " [1] The proceedings of this State in relation
to the five per cent. impost," says the late Chief Justice,
" were in perfect accordance with her political creed, published in May, 1776, and reiterated in October, 1782. The
grant in the terms proposed, interfered very materially with
'the internal police and conduct' of State affairs ; for the
impost proposed, was to be collected within the state by
officers not appointed by its authority and not under its con-
trol. The discussion of State rights, which grew out of it,
confirmed the citizens of the State in their original creed.
The arguments of Mr. Howell, in favor of these rights,
acquired a greater force from the apparent attempt in Congress
to put him down because of his opinions honestly and earnestly expressed. .   Is it not more than probable that the
state right doctrine so eloquently urged by Mr. Howell, in-
flamed and gave strength to the prejudices which imbued a
majority of the citizens of Rhode Island to oppose that Constitution, when it was proposed for their acceptance ? "

The price paid by the American states for independence,
in addition to the blood shed, was impoverishment and ex-
haustion. The expense of carrying on the war had been
vast : currency had depreciated : taxation had been heavy ;
and the channels of industry had been greatly disturbed,

[1] Staples, 429.

and, in some cases, destroyed. The flow of specie from the United States was alarming. The imports from Great Britain in 1784 and 1785 amounted to $30,000,000, while the exports thither did not exceed $9,000,000, leaving a balance of $21,000,000 against us.[1] In some states laws to stay the collection of debts were passed; in others tender laws were made, or enactments to enable the transfer of property in settlement of debts. In Massachusetts and New Hampshire an insurrectionary spirit was rife, and in the former the famous Shay's Rebellion was only put down by the shedding of blood, and after the sessions of the courts had been interfered with, and other excesses committed. Rhode Island was no exception to the rule, and she was worse, rather than better off than her sister states, as her sufferings during the Revolutionary War had reduced her to sad straits. For three years during the war a British army had occupied the island of Rhode Island and some other portions of the state, and a British fleet had held the mouth of Narragansett Bay, thus practically sealing up the state. Bristol and Warren had been partially destroyed. Commerce had been annihilated.[2] The ancient and once wealthy town of Newport, which had rivalled Boston and New York in commercial importance, was ruined, and out of nearly one hundred and fifty sail she sent to sea in 1774, three only were at sea in March, 1782.[3] "Near two thousand persons,"[4] wrote Governor Greene from Providence, in 1779, "who have been driven from Rhode Island by the enemy, are now among us, the greater part of whom subsist by charity. The most obdurate heart would relent to see old age and childhood,

[1] Pitkin's Statistical View of the Commerce of the United States, 30, 31.
[2] Staples, 182, 200, 212, 213, 220; S R. I. Col. Rec., 498-500.
[3] Howell to Gov. Greene: Staples, 382.
[4] S R. I. Col. Rec., 500.

from comfortable circumstances, reduced to the necessity
of begging for a morsel of bread ; and even that they cannot
often obtain ; not for the want of a sympathetic feeling in
the inhabitants for their distresses, but merely from their
inability to relieve them." In the same year the Board of
War wrote :—"[1] The State is burdened with debt, reduced to
poverty,   and we are almost upon the verge of a
famine."

In the terrible pressure succeeding the struggle for independence, some of the states again resorted to emissions
of paper money in the hope of relief. Among these were
New Jersey, Pennsylvania, Georgia, North Carolina and
South Carolina. When the Bank of the United States refused to receive Pennsylvania's bills as of equal value with
its own, the state repealed the bank's act of incorporation.[2] The Rhode Island General Assembly, early in 1786,
had granted assent to Congress to enact an impost law, and
at the same time had refused to grant a petition for an emission of paper money. At the election in April of that year
the opponents of the impost and the friends of paper money
coalesced and carried the state.[3] An emission of £100,000
in paper currency was then voted, and drastic measures were
adopted to secure its being received in payment of debts and
in exchange for merchandise. During the summer and early
autumn of 1786 great confusion was caused by the attempt
to enforce these harsh and unjust measures, but in the
famous case of Trevett vs. Weeden, tried in October of that
year, the court, composed of judges, some of whom were
avowed paper money men, and all of whom had been elected
by the General Assembly that passed the acts, unanimously
pronounced some of their provisions unconstitutional. After
this decision stores which had been closed, were re-opened,

[1] Staples, 221.   [2] 1 Bancroft, 233-237.   [3] Staples, 540.

and trade went on much as usual.[1] One would suppose from
what has been written relating to paper money in Rhode
Island, and the effect of it upon her action in regard to the
federal constitution, that she was the only state that had
issued such currency, and that those states that had not
emitted any since the Revolution, were prompt and unanimous in their adoption of the federal compact.

The Confederation had proved weak and inefficient.
Trade was languishing, and there was no uniform system
for commercial regulation. Public credit had sunk to the
lowest ebb, and anything worthy the name of government
was more delusive than real. Every one agreed that something should be done to strengthen the government, and to
this end the State of Virginia, in January, 1786, proposed a
convention of states to be held at Annapolis in the follow-

[1] The late venerable Wilkins Updike (brother of the secretary of the Rhode Island
convention that ratified the federal constitution), in his History of the Narragansett
Church, at page 250, in writing of the Hon. Joseph Hazard, says :—" He was elected to
many important offices by the people, and sustained them with honor. Although a determined partisan, he never permitted his political attachments to sway him from the principles of right. His motto was ' to do right, and let consequences take care of themselves.'
He was on the bench of the Supreme Court of the State, when the General Assembly
enacted the celebrated 'Paper Money Laws' of 1780, and was one of the paper money party.
As the party put the judges into office, it was expected that the judges would support the
party. But when the question of the constitutionality of those laws came before the court
for decision in the case of Trevett vs. Weeden, in which cause Gen. Varnum made his
great and eloquent effort, this court stood firm in the defence of the cause of law in their
country, and declared the Paper Money Tender Laws unconstitutional and void. Their
fiery partisans in the General Assembly ordered the court to be arraigned before them for
a contempt of legislative power, and they were required to give their respective reasons
for overthrowing the laws of the Legislature that had *created* them."

When the five judges of the " Superior Court of Judicature, Court of Assize, and
General Gaol-Delivery " were summoned before the General Assembly, at its September
session, 1786, to render their reasons for adjudging an act of the General Assembly unconstitutional and void, only three of them attended, the other two being unwell, so they
were directed to appear at the October session. At this latter session of the General
Assembly, according to Gen. Varnum's report of the case of Trevett vs. Weeden, and
the case of the judges growing out of the same, at page 43, Judge Hazard delivered the
following remarks :—" My brethren have so fully declared my sentiments upon this occa-

ing September, for the purpose of framing such regulations of
trade as might be judged necessary to promote the general
interest,[1] and our so-called paper money General Assembly,
at its June session in that year, promptly elected delegates.[2] The result of the discussion in Congress on the
report of the Annapolis Convention was the passage in
February, 1787, of a resolution calling for a convention of
delegates to meet at Philadelphia in May, for the sole and
express purpose of revising the articles of confederation
and reporting such alterations and provisions therein as
should render them adequate to the exigencies of the gov-

sion, that I have nothing to add by way of argument. It gives me pain that the conduct
of the Court seems to have met the displeasure of the Administration. But their obligations were of too sacred a nature for them to aim at pleasing but in the line of their duty.

"It is well known that my sentiments have fully accorded with the general system
of the Legislature in emitting the paper currency; but I never did, I never will, depart
from the character of an honest man, to support any measures, however agreeable in themselves. If there could have been a prepossession in my mind, it must have been in favour
of the act of the General Assembly; but it was not possible to resist the force of conviction. The opinion I gave upon the trial was dictated by the energy of truth; I thought
it right—I still think so. Be it as it may, we derived our understanding from the Almighty,
and to Him only are we accountable for our judgment."

General Varnum, in referring to the result of Trevett vs. Weeden, in his report of that
case, says on page 37:—"The consequences of the foregoing determination were imme-
diately felt. The shops and stores were generally opened, and business assumed a cheer-
ful aspect. Few were the exceptions to a general congratulation, and lavish indeed were
the praises bestowed upon the Court. The dread and the idea of informations were
banished together, while a most perfect confidence was placed in judicial security. The
paper currency obtained a more extensive circulation, as every one found himself at
liberty to receive or refuse it. The markets, which had been illy supplied, were now
amply furnished, and the spirit of industry was generally diffused."

The forcing acts or penal laws respecting paper money were formally repealed by the
General Assembly of Rhode Island at its December session, 1786. R. I. Acts and
Resolves, Dec. Sess. 1786, p. 23.

[1] The importance of the Annapolis Convention is portrayed by Bancroft in these words:—
"Congress having confessedly failed to find ways and means for carrying on the government, the convention which had been called at Annapolis became the ground of hope for
the nation." Vol. I., 267.

[2] Staples, 592.

ernment and the preservation of the union.[1] Thus originated the famous convention which formed the present federal constitution.

Much stress has been laid upon the fact that Rhode Island was not represented in that convention ; but that she was not, seems to have been due to accident rather than to any party bias or design, notwithstanding that the party sometimes called the paper money party, sometimes the country party, and sometimes the anti-federal party, then was, and for many years afterwards continued to be, in power. The General Assembly in March, 1787, voted not to send delegates, but this body had been elected the year previous, before the convention had been called. In April, 1787, a new General Assembly was chosen when the question of the Philadelphia Convention was before the electors, and at its session in May, the House of Representatives by two majority voted in favor of sending delegates, while the Senate non-concurred by the same majority, two Senators being absent, who, if present, would have increased the majority to four. The next month the matter came up again, when, strange to relate, the action of the two bodies was exactly reversed, the house, composed of sixty-four members, voting by a majority of seventeen against sending delegates, and the Senate, consisting of the governor, deputy governor and ten assistants or senators, by a majority of five being in favor of sending delegates.[2] Thus both houses of the so-called paper money party, which had been elected with a full knowledge that a convention was to be held in Philadelphia, had within two months of their election, voted for and against, sending delegates, each house when it reversed

[1] Journals of Congress, published by Folwell, 1801. Vol. 12, pp. 12—14.
[2] Staples, 572.

its former vote, doing so by a much larger majority than marked its original action. In both May and June the members were identically the same. No explanation of these contradictory votes has come down to us, but whatever it may have been, it effectually dissipates the loose assertion so often indulged in, that the prominent party in the General Assembly was from the start, bitterly opposed to taking any part in the constitutional convention. Moreover it had sent delegates to the Annapolis Convention, and the Philadelphia Convention was likewise called simply to amend the articles of confederation, even the members themselves of that convention not dreaming till after they had been in session for weeks that anything else than such amendment might be the result of their labors. Nine days elapsed after the Philadelphia Convention met before a bare quorum could be secured, and, sitting with closed doors, it concluded its work September 17th. It consisted of sixty-five members, ten of whom never attended. Thirty-nine signed the constitution, and sixteen who attended did not sign. Although the vote of eleven states represented on the last day of the convention, was recorded as unanimous in favor of it, the vote of each state being determined by a majority of its delegates, yet it is to be noted that, owing to absence or refusal, the full delegations of but three states actually signed the instrument.[1]

Great opposition greeted the new constitution. With our century of experience under it, we, who have realized its beneficent workings, may well wonder at the hostility it encountered, but it came not from any one state alone, or from any particular class in the community. Patriots, orators, and statesmen, men whose fame has made

[1] Elliot's Debates on the Federal Constitution, 124, 125.

their names as familiar as household words, refused to give it their support. In Virginia the opponents were especially distinguished. Among them were Patrick Henry, a former governor of the state, whose burning eloquence is known wherever the English language is spoken ; Thomas Nelson and Benjamin Harrison, both signers of the Declaration of Independence and ex-governors, the latter of whom was ancestor of two presidents of the United States; Richard Henry Lee and George Mason, both violent opponents of paper money, the former having been president of Congress, and the latter a member of the constitutional convention, and as such had refused to sign the instrument ; and then too, there was James Monroe, afterwards president of the United States. Among the Massachusetts opponents were Elbridge Gerry and Nathan Dane.[1] Gerry was a signer of the Declaration of Independence, and he had refused to sign the constitution in the convention that framed it. Subsequently he became governor of Massachusetts and vice-president of the United States. Dane was the framer of the famous Ordinance of 1787 for the government of the North West Territory providing for the exclusion of slavery. In New York the opposition was extremely violent. A majority of her delegates had opposed the constitution in the convention, and had withdrawn from that body before its adoption there.[2] The governor of the state, Gen. George Clinton, was active in his disapproval.[3] With such an array of great names, and I have mentioned but a few of the opponents, it is idle to impute to paper money the cause of the hostility. Some objected for one reason, some for another, but much of the opposition sprang from the absence from the

---

[1] 2 Bancroft, 226 et post ; 300 et post. 5 Elliot, 553.   [2] 1 Elliot, 480 et post.

[3] 2 Bancroft, 340 et post, 469.

instrument of a declaration of rights asserting and securing
from encroachment the great principles of civil and religious
liberty and the inalienable rights of the people.[1] Indeed,
Thomas Jefferson at one time wrote :—"[2] I wish with all my
soul that the nine first conventions may accept the new constitution, to secure to us the good it contains ; but I equally
wish that the four latest, whichever they may be, may refuse
to accede to it till a declaration of rights be annexed ; but,"
he added, "no objection to the new form must produce a
schism in our union."

Of the state conventions called to ratify the constitution
there were but three in which the delegates were unanimous
in its favor, and two of these, Georgia and New Jersey, were
so-called paper money states, having made emissions of that
currency since the close of the Revolution.

In the Massachusetts Convention it was extremely doubt-
ful whether the friends or the opponents of the constitution
were in the ascendancy.[3] Bancroft tells us that "the rural
population were disinclined to a change."[4] For nearly a
month discussion continued in that body, and then only by
the gentlest and most conciliatory persuasion, and after recommending nine amendments, was the instrument adopted
by a majority of but nineteen in a convention of over three
hundred and fifty members.[5] It should be remembered that
Massachusetts had issued no paper money since the Revolution, and when in May, 1786, a petition for an emission of
that currency was presented, out of one hundred and eighteen members in her House of Representatives it received
but nineteen votes ;[6] so the opposition in that state could

[1] 2 Bancroft, 227, 227 et post.
[2] 2 Bancroft, 275.
[3] 2 Bancroft, 259.
[4] 2 Bancroft, 259.
[5] 2 Elliot, 178 et post ; 2 Bancroft, 261.
[6] 1 Bancroft, 230 et post.

hardly be attributed to paper money. Every county west of Essex, Suffolk, Plymouth and Barnstable, or the extreme eastern tier, cast a majority against adopting the constitution.[1] The majority of the delegates of Bristol County, which bounds this state on the east, was opposed to it. In the great County of Worcester, as large territorially as the whole State of Rhode Island, and which bounds this state on the north, forty-three delegates were opposed to it, and only eight favored it.[2] Surely, Rhode Island was not so much worse than her neighbors, after all.

New Hampshire, another New England state not ranked as paper money, had delayed sending delegates to the constitutional convention for a month after the time fixed for the day of meeting, and her state convention, after taking a recess of four months, ratified by but eleven majority, and only after recommending twelve amendments.[3]

In Virginia the contest lasted for more than three weeks, when adoption was secured by eighty-nine to seventy-nine, a majority of ten, and that too with recommendations of amendment.[4]

In the great state of New York, where the impost question was the stumbling block, the convention was in session for more than a month, and ratification was finally carried by thirty to twenty-seven, a bare majority of three; and to obtain this result a recommendation of a series of amendments had to be included.[5]

---

[1] 2 Elliot, 178 et post. The present County of Norfolk then formed part of Suffolk County: 3 Barry's History of Massachusetts, 208.

[2] 2 Elliot, 180 et post.

[3] 1 Bancroft, 276; 2 Bancroft, 277 et post, and 318. 1 Curtis's Constitutional History of the United States, 328.

[4] 3 Elliot, 1, 657, 662.

[5] 2 Elliot, 205, 413.

In North Carolina a convention was called in July, 1788, and after remaining in session for three weeks and agreeing upon a long declaration of rights and twenty-six amendments, it voted by a hundred majority to adjourn without either ratifying or rejecting, but desiring that some further action should be taken to amend the instrument before voting to adopt it. Seventeen months later, on November 21, 1789, she ratified it, being the last state but our own to do so.[1]

Rhode Island, therefore, was, by no means, the only state where deep rooted opposition to the constitution existed. During all this exciting period the question of calling a convention in Rhode Island had from time to time been introduced into our General Assembly, and seven times had been voted down.

The country party was in power, and we have seen that elsewhere as well as in Rhode Island, it was the rural population that hated change. The action of the other states had been closely watched and their objections noted. One thing strikes a Rhode Islander very peculiarly in regard to the adoption of the federal constitution. The people were not to vote directly upon it, but only second-hand through delegates to a state convention. No amendment to our state constitution, even at this day, can be adopted without a majority of three-fifths of all the votes cast, the voting being directly on the proposition, and a hundred years ago no state was more democratic in its notions than Rhode Island. Although the Philadelphia Convention had provided that the federal constitution should be ratified in the different states by conventions of delegates elected by the people for that purpose, upon the call of the General Assembly, yet this did not

[1] 4 Elliot, 242, 251.

accord with the Rhode Island idea, so in February, 1788, the
General Assembly voted to submit the question whether the
constitution of the United States should be adopted, to the
voice of the people to be expressed at the polls on the fourth
Monday in March.[1] The federalists fearing they would be
out-voted, largely abstained from voting, so the vote stood two
hundred and thirty-seven for the constitution, and two thousand seven hundred and eight against it, there being about four
thousand voters in the state at that time.[2] Governor Collins,
in a letter to the president of Congress written a few days
after the vote was taken, gives the feeling then existing in
Rhode Island, in this wise :—"Although this state has been
singular from her sister states in the mode of collecting the
sentiments of the people upon the constitution, it was not done
with the least design to give any offence to the respectable
body who composed the convention, or a disregard to the recommendation of Congress, but upon pure republican principles, founded upon that basis of all governments originally
derived from the body of the people at large. And although,
sir, the majority has been so great against adopting the Constitution, yet the people, in general, conceive that it may
contain some necessary articles which could well be added
and adapted to the present confederation. They are sensible that the present powers invested with Congress are incom-
petent for the great national government of the Union, and
would heartily acquiesce in granting sufficient authority to
that body to make, exercise and enforce laws throughout the
states, which would tend to regulate commerce and impose
duties and excise, whereby Congress might establish funds
for discharging the public debt."[3]

A majority of the voters of the country was undoubtedly

[1] Staples, 589.   [2] Staples, 500.   [3] 10 R. I. Col. Rec., 291.

against the constitution, but convention after convention was carried by the superior address and management of its friends.[1] Rhode Island lacked great men, who favored the constitution, to lead her. In Virginia, for the constitution, were George Washington and James Madison, John Marshall, and Edmund Randolph, the governor of the state. James Monroe wrote to Thomas Jefferson :—"Be assured, Washington's influence carried this government."[2] Gouverneur Morris, in a letter to Washington himself, says :—"I have observed that your name to the new Constitution has been of infinite service. Indeed, I am convinced that if you had not attended that Convention, and the same paper had been handed out to the world, it would have met with a colder reception, with fewer and weaker advocates, and with more and more strenuous opponents. As it is, should the idea prevail that you will not accept the Presidency, it would prove fatal in many parts."[3] And yet, with this great leadership in Virginia, the constitution in that state was adopted

[1] Bancroft, 258, 265, 200, 277, 317, 340, 354, 300, 400, 178, 405 et post. 4 Hildreth's History of the United States, 35. Chief Justice Marshall, himself a member of the Philadelphia Convention, says :—"So balanced were parties in some of them," (i. e. the states) "that even after the subject had been discussed for a considerable time, the fate of the constitution could scarcely be conjectured; and so small, in many instances, was the majority in its favor, as to afford strong ground for the opinion that had the influence of character been removed, the intrinsic merits of the instrument would not have secured its adoption. Indeed, it is scarcely to be doubted that in some of the adopting states, a majority of the people were in the opposition. In all of them, the numerous amendments which were proposed, demonstrate the reluctance with which the new government was accepted; and that a dread of dismemberment, not an approbation of the particular system under consideration, had induced an acquiescence in it." 5 Marshall's Washington, 132.

The following sentence from Bancroft shows the bitterness of the opposition in some quarters. Referring to Pennsylvania's ratification, he writes :—"The ratification gave unbounded satisfaction to all Pennsylvania on the eastern side of the Susquehanna; beyond that river loud murmurs were mingled with threats of resistance in arms." 2 Bancroft, 252.

[2] 2 Bancroft, 317.

[3] 1 Elliot, 500.

by but ten majority, after sundry amendments had been recommended. In New York there were Alexander Hamilton, John Jay and Robert R. Livingston for the constitution; and in Massachusetts, Theophilus Parsons, Theodore Sedgwick and Fisher Ames, Ex-Governor Bowdoin and Generals Heath and Lincoln ; and then, too, there were John Hancock and Samuel Adams ; the latter two having been far from strong for the constitution at the start, were all the better adapted to carry others to the conviction at which they finally arrived.

Who was there of towering prominence in Rhode Island for the constitution, to lead the people at that trying period ? Gen. Nathaniel Greene had removed to Georgia where he had died. Gen. James M. Varnum, a gallant Revolutionary officer, an eloquent lawyer, and a member of Congress, might, perhaps, under other circumstances, have exerted much influence for good, but he removed to Illinois in June, 1788, having been appointed by Congress one of the judges of the North West Territory ; and there he died in 1789, at the early age of forty years.[1] A thorough partisan, he ruined any influence he might have had with Rhode Island anti-federalists by writing a violent letter to the president of the Philadelphia Convention denouncing the General Assembly and many citizens of the state.[2]

In some close states, where the leaders were wise, gentle means were resorted to. Thus Bancroft tells us :—" The federalists of Philadelphia had handled their opponents roughly ; the federalists of Massachusetts resolved never in debate to fail in gentleness and courtesy."[3] In regard to the Virginia Convention he writes :—" The discussions had been temperately conducted till just at the last," and then he pro-

[1] Updike's Memories of the Rhode Island Bar, 145 et post.   [2] 5 Elliot, 577.
[3] 2 Bancroft, 261.

ceeds to narrate an ebullition by Patrick Henry. Again he
says :—"After the vote was taken, the successful party were
careful not to ruffle their opponents by exultation."[1] In
Rhode Island the federalists, instead of trying to convert
their opponents by "gentleness and courtesy," as in Massachusetts, heaped abuse upon them, like Varnum ; and the
whole federal party of the country joined in the same spirit
of denunciation. John Temple, the British consul-gen-
eral to the United States, wrote from New York to the
Marquis of Carmarthen as early as June 7, 1787 :—"The
little state of Rhode Island hath already gone so retrograde
to the articles of confederation, and to the subsequent orders
and doings of congress, and having not thought proper to
send delegates to the convention, it is already seriously
talked of, the annihilating of Rhode Island as a state, and to
divide that territory (I mean the government of it) between
Massachusetts and Connecticut."[2] George Ticknor Curtis,
writing of the opposition in Rhode Island, says :—"[3]Ridicule
and scorn were heaped upon them from all quarters of the
country, and ardent zealots of the Federal press urged the
adoption of the advice which they said the grand seignior
had given to the king of Spain with respect to the refractory
states of Holland, namely, to send his men with shovels and
pickaxes, and throw them all into the sea." This being the
treatment allotted to the people of Rhode Island, would it
be strange if it reacted and made them more tenacious and
persistent in their course?

The requisite number of states having ratified the constitution, a government was formed under it April 30, 1789.
Our General Assembly, at its September session in that

[1] 2 Bancroft, 311, 310.   [2] 2 Bancroft, 126.   [3] 1 Curtis, 605.

year, sent a long letter[1] to Congress explanatory of the situation in Rhode Island, and its importance warrants my quoting a part of it. "The people of this state from its first settlement," ran the letter, "have been accustomed and strongly attached to a democratical form of government. They have viewed in the new constitution an approach, though perhaps but small, toward that form of government from which we have lately dissolved our connection at so much hazard and expense of life and treasure,—they have seen with pleasure the administration thereof from the most important trusts downward, committed to men who have highly merited and in whom the people of the United States place *unbounded confidence*. Yet, even on this circumstance, in itself so fortunate, they have apprehended danger by way of precedent. Can it be thought strange, then, that with these impressions, they should wait to see the proposed system organized and in operation, to see what further checks and securities would be agreed to and established by way of *amendments*, before they would adopt it as a constitution of government for themselves and their posterity? These amendments we believe have already afforded some relief and satisfaction to the minds of the people of this state. And we earnestly look for the time, when they may with clearness and safety, be again united with their sister states under a constitution and form of government so well poised, as neither to need alteration or be liable thereto by a majority only of nine states out of *thirteen*, a circumstance which may possibly take place against the sense of a majority of the people of the United States. We are sensible of the extremes to which democratical government is sometimes liable; something of which we have lately experienced, but we esteem them tem-

[1] to R. I. Col. Rec., 356.

3

porary and partial evils, compared with the loss of liberty
and the rights of a free people."

Rhode Island never supposed she could stand alone. In
the words of her General Assembly in the letter just referred to :—" They know themselves to be a handful, com-
paratively viewed." This letter, as well as a former one I
have quoted from, showed that she, like New Hampshire,
Massachusetts, New York, Virginia, and North Carolina,
hoped to see the constitution amended. Like the latter
state she believed in getting the amendments *before* ratification, and so strong was the pressure for amendments that
at the very first session of Congress a series of amendments
was introduced and passed for ratification by the states, and
Rhode Island, though the last state to adopt the constitution, was the ninth state to ratify the first ten amendments
to that instrument now in force ; ratifying both constitution
and amendments at practically the same time.[1] One can
hardly wonder at the pressure for amendments to the original constitution when the amendments have to be resorted
to for provisions that Congress shall make no law respecting
an establishment of religion, or prohibiting the free use
thereof, or abridging the freedom of speech, or of the press,
or the right of the people peaceably to assemble and to

[1] Hickey's Constitution of the United States, p. 34.

The constitution of the United States was ratified, not by the people voting directly
upon the question of ratification, as is the case with amendments to our Rhode Island
state constitution, but by conventions of delegates elected by the people, and became
operative upon the states ratifying it, when ratified by the conventions of nine states.
Amendments, however, were, by the terms of the constitution, to be ratified by state
legislatures, and when ratified by the legislatures of three-fourths of the states were to
be binding upon all the states even though the legislatures of some of the states never
ratified them at all.

The Rhode Island Convention ratified the federal constitution, May 29, 1790, and the
legislature of Rhode Island ratified the first ten amendments June 15, 1790, being at
the first session of the General Assembly after the ratification of the constitution.

petition the government for a redress of grievances ; that
excessive bail should not be required, nor excessive fines
imposed, nor cruel and unusual punishments inflicted ; for
right of trial by jury in civil cases ; and for other highly
important provisions.[1]

North Carolina, despairing of obtaining the desired
amendments, ratified the constitution November 21, 1789,
and entered the constitutional union, so Rhode Island
stood alone.   How long could she continue so to stand, and
could she, single-handed, hope to obtain amendments before
ratification ?

The two leaders of the dominant party in Rhode Island
were John Collins, the governor of the state, and Jonathan
J. Hazard, a member of the House of Representatives from
South Kingstown.   Governor Collins had been patriotic
during the war, had been a member of Congress for five
years, and was a thoroughly honest and high-toned man.[2]
Jonathan J. Hazard took an early and decided stand in favor
of liberty in the struggle for independence.   In 1776 he
appeared in the General Assembly from Charlestown, and
the next year he was elected paymaster of the Continental
Battalion and joined the army in New Jersey   In 1778 he
was re-elected a member of the General Assembly and constituted one of the Council of War ; and he continued a
member of the House most of the time during the Revolution.   He was likewise a delegate in Congress in 1787 and
1788.   He was a natural orator, with a ready command of language, and was subtle and ingenious in debate.   He was for
a long time the idol of the country interest, manager of the

[1] See Appendix.

[2] Appleton's Cyclopaedia of Am. Biog.   See also Governor Collins's Correspondence in
Staples, and in R. I. Col. Records.

state, leader of the legislature, and, indeed, the political
dictator of Rhode Island. He was the most efficient leader
of the paper money party in 1786 and their ablest debater
in the General Assembly. Later he was the leader of the anti-
federalists and a fiery opponent of the constitution.[1]

The situation in Rhode Island had become critical indeed.
The Congress of the new United States had declared that
after January 15, 1790, Rhode Island was to be treated as a
foreigner and a stranger. Newport, Providence, Bristol and
Westerly were clamorous for the constitution. Something
must be done and that quickly. In October, 1789, before
North Carolina had ratified, the motion for a convention had
been voted down in the Rhode Island General Assembly by a
vote of thirty-nine to seventeen, but when that body next met
in January, 1790, the aspect of affairs had vastly changed. Five
days after the beginning of the January session the House by
five majority voted to call a convention, but the Senate
non-concurred, and passed an act requesting the freemen
to instruct their representatives in the General Assembly
whether a convention should be called. In this the House
refused to concur by fourteen majority, and thus matters
stood when the Assembly adjourned until the next day.
Great excitement prevailed on Sunday and the unusual spec-
tacle of the General Assembly sitting on the Sabbath and
the great interest in the measure under consideration drew a
throng to the State House. Another bill for a convention to
be held March 1st was introduced in the House and passed by
thirty-two to eleven. About noon the vote was taken in the
Senate on concurrence, and, as the senators were evenly
divided, all eyes were turned towards Governor Collins, as
with him rested the decision. After reviewing the proceed-

[1] Updike's History of the Narragansett Church, 348 et post.

ings in relation to a convention and the action of other
states, he concluded by referring to the peculiar situation
of this state and cast his vote for concurrence; and so it
was settled that a convention to consider the question of
ratifying the federal constitution was to be called. In
view of the progress made, the time for treating Rhode
Island as an alien was deferred by Congress until April 15th.[1]

February 8th, the delegates were elected, and the convention assembled at South Kingstown on the day designated,
all of the seventy members being present. Forty-two were
members of the General Assembly, comprising the leaders
of both houses, among them Jonathan J. Hazard. Four had
held the office of deputy-governor, five had been delegates
to the Continental Congress, and the whole constituted a
thoroughly representative body.[2] The convention sat from
March 1st to March 6th making little progress, when it adjourned to meet at Newport on the fourth Monday in May.[3]
During the recess all the leverage and influence that could
be brought to bear to affect votes, were put in operation.
One of the most remarkable results of the adjournment was
the changed attitude of Jonathan J. Hazard, who had up to
that time been the leader and forefront of the opposition.
Though he voted against ratification to the last, yet his
opposition had become so neutralized that he ceased longer
to take an active part.[4]

The convention re-assembled at Newport May 25th, and as
the State House was utterly insufficient for the accommoda-
tion of the great numbers that manifested their interest by
their attendance, the convention removed to the Second
Baptist Church, where for three days the great debate went

[1] Staples, 625-630.   [2] Staples, 633, 634.   [3] Staples, 650, 650.
[4] Updike's History of the Narragansett Church, 329.   Staples, 663-666.

on, until at last on Saturday, May 29th, at twenty minutes
past five in the afternoon, the vote was taken and the constitution was ratified by a vote of thirty-four to thirty-two,
and at the same time a series of amendments was recommended.[1] The *Providence Gazette* of June 5, 1790, tells
us :—"Many more members of the convention were convinced of the propriety of so adopting the constitution, and
the majority would, it appears, have been much larger, had
not a number of the members been restricted by instruc-
tions. Had it been compatible with the public good to have
adjourned the decision for a short time only, these instruc-
tions would, undoubtedly, have been reversed ; but as there
was a majority for the adoption, and the situation of the
state extremely critical, it was deemed expedient to take the
question." The news of the ratification arrived in Providence by express at eleven o'clock at night and was immedi-
ately announced by the ringing of bells and the firing of can-
non.[2] Rhode Island speedily elected senators and representatives to Congress, and thus became a member of the
constitutional union.

Rhode Island has been attacked and abused for her tardiness, beyond all bounds of reason. She was a sovereign
state, the mistress of her own destiny, and she had both a
technical and a moral right to pursue such course as she
deemed for her own best good. She had violated no right
of her sister states ; she had broken no pledges to them.
On the other hand all the states had solemnly pledged their
faith that the union formed under the articles of confederation should be perpetual, and that no alteration should at
any time be made in any of those articles unless confirmed

---

[1] Staples, 659, 672 'ss'.   [2] Arnold's History of Rhode Island, 562.
[2] *Providence Gazette*, June 5, 1790.

by the legislature of every state. However satisfactory the express provisions of the constitution might have been, yet it was provided that three-fourths of the states might amend them at pleasure, and, truly, the conferring of such power was a leap in the dark. Rhode Island never opposed union. On the contrary she always favored it, being among the first to propose it; and as we have seen she was the second of all the states to instruct her delegates in Congress to ratify the articles of confederation providing for a perpetual union. She had performed her duty as well as most of the states, and in the struggle for independence she had been second to none. Her state sovereignty had been planted in exile and fostered by persecution: its corner-stone rested on soul-liberty; and its preservation and integrity had been assured only by her sturdy resistance to the aggressions of her neighbors, and she was unwilling to transmit to posterity either that sovereignty impaired, or with the right to impair it vested in three-fourths of her sister states. To the many writers failing in a just perception of the true state of affairs, that have heaped reproaches upon Rhode Island, especially during the last few years embraced within the centennial period of our government, I would commend these words of George Bancroft:—"Neither of the two states which lingered behind remonstrated against the establishment of a new government before their consent; nor did they ask the United States to wait for them. The worst that can be said of them is, that they were late in arriving."[1]

Having once entered the constitutional union, Rhode Island has loyally adhered to it, and the blood of her sons has been

---

[1] 2 Bancroft, 350.

lavishly shed, and the money in her treasury has been boun-
tifully expended in preserving it.   Rhode Island may be conservative and peculiar, but, if a tree is to be judged by its
fruit, where can a richer harvest be found than here within
her borders?   Thriving towns, cities and villages stud her
rugged soil.   Her rivers on their course from the hill-side to
the sea everywhere pay tribute to industry.   Her whirling
spindles and flying shuttles produce fabrics of surpassing
excellence.   Her forges and her workshops furnish alike the
most ponderous machines and the most delicate mechanisms.
The skill of her artisans, in unrivalled profusion, fashion
forms of beauty out of silver and gold.   Churches and
school-houses abound, educating for this world and pointing
onward and upward to the next.   Literally in no state in
the union are there so many inhabitants to the square mile
of land area, as here upon her territory.[1]   Carpers may cavil
at her, detractors may traduce,—but as well might they strive
to pluck the love of soul-liberty from the hearts of men, as
permanently to be-little her character or obscure her fame.

[1] By the Census of the United States for 1880, Rhode Island had 251.87 inhabitants to a
square mile of land surface, while Massachusetts, the next most densely populated state,
had but 221.78 inhabitants to a square mile of land surface.   Compendium of the Tenth
Census of the United States, 1880.   Part 2, 1113.

APPENDIX.

THE statement has sometimes been made that inasmuch as the United States possessed no powers except those conferred by the constitution, the prohibitions contained in a number of the first ten amendments of that instrument were practically nugatory, and therefore unnecessary. The wisdom of our fathers, however, in insisting upon those prohibitions, would seem to be beyond question in view of the fact that what are termed the incidental, or implied, or auxiliary powers embraced in the constitution, have proved to be the ones most open to dispute and fraught with the greatest danger.

Chief Justice Marshall, in McCulloch vs. Maryland, in the United States Supreme Court, 4 Wheaton's Rep., 407, said :—"A constitution, to contain an accurate detail of all the subdivisions of which its great powers will admit, and of all the means by which they may be carried into execution, would partake of the prolixity of a legal code, and could scarcely be embraced by the human mind. It would probably never be understood by the public. Its nature, therefore, requires that only its great outlines should be marked, its important objects designated, and the minor ingredients which compose those objects be deduced from the nature of the objects themselves." Mr. Justice Strong, in the famous Legal Tender Cases, so called, also in the United States Supreme Court, 12 Wallace's Rep , 532, used these words :—" We do not expect to find in a constitution minute details. It is necessarily brief and comprehensive. It prescribes outlines, leaving the filling up to be deduced from the outlines." Later in the same opinion, on page 550, this language occurs:—"We are accustomed to speak for mere convenience of the express and implied powers conferred upon Congress. But in fact the auxiliary powers, those necessary and appropriate to the execution of other powers singly described, are as expressly given as is the power to declare war, or to establish uniform laws on the subject of bankruptcy. They are not catalogued, no list of them is made. but they are grouped in the last clause of section eight of the first article, and granted in the same words in which all other

4

powers are granted to Congress." The last clause of section eight of the first article of the federal constitution, referred to, reads as follows:— "And to make all laws which shall be necessary and proper for carrying into execution the foregoing powers, and all other powers vested by this constitution in the government of the United States, or in any department or officer thereof."

The wide divergence of opinion often existing among the judges of the United States Supreme Court, upon questions of constitutional law, engenders grave doubts whether the federal constitution has not at times been construed to mean exactly the reverse of what its framers intended. This divergence is strikingly illustrated in the decisions relating to paper money, or legal tender, so called. In 1870, the United States Supreme Court decided that the Acts of Congress known as the Legal Tender Acts, were unconstitutional when applied to private contracts made before their passage; that is to say, that Congress could not constitutionally pass a law making paper money a legal tender for the payment of debts contracted before the passage of such law. Hepburn vs. Griswold, 8 Wallace's Rep., 603. In 1871, the same court, with a somewhat changed membership, overruled the decision of the year before and decided precisely the contrary. Legal Tender Cases, 12 Wallace's Rep., 457.

The utter contradiction and confusion often attending judicial construction of constitutional provisions, is signally displayed in Juilliard vs. Greenman, another Legal Tender Case, decided in the United States Supreme Court in 1884, and reported in 110 U. S. Sup. Ct. Rep., 421. Mr. Justice Gray, in delivering the opinion of the court in that case, on page 447, used this language:—" It appears to us to follow, as a logical and necessary consequence, that Congress has the power to issue the obligations of the United States in such form, and to impress upon them such qualities as currency for the purchase of merchandise and the payment of debts, as accord with the usage of sovereign governments. The power, as incident to the power of borrowing money and issuing bills or notes of the government for money borrowed, of impressing upon those bills or notes the quality of being a legal tender for the payment of private debts, was a power universally understood to belong to sovereignty, in Europe and America, at the time of the framing and adoption of the Constitution of the United States. * * * The power of issuing bills of credit, and making them, at the discretion of the legislature, a tender in payment of private debts, had long been exercised in this country by the several Colonies and States; and during the Revolutionary War the States,

APPENDIX. 43

upon the recommendation of the Congress of the Confederation, had
made the bills issued by Congress a legal tender. The exercise of this
power not being prohibited to Congress by the Constitution, it is included
in the power expressly granted to borrow money on the credit of the
United States."

On the other hand, Mr. Justice Field, in delivering a dissenting opinion
in the same case, page 466, *et post*, spoke in this wise :—" But beyond and
above all the objections which I have stated to the decision recognizing a
power in Congress to impart the legal tender quality to the notes of the
government, is my objection to the rule of construction adopted by the
court to reach its conclusions, a rule which fully carried out would change
the whole nature of our Constitution and break down the barriers which
separate a government of limited from one of unlimited powers. When
the Constitution came before the conventions of the several States for
adoption, apprehension existed that other powers than those designated
might be claimed; and it led to the first ten amendments. When these
were presented to the States they were preceded by a preamble stating that
the conventions of a number of the States had at the time of adopting the
Constitution expressed a desire, ' in order to prevent misconception or
abuse of its powers, that further declaratory and restrictive clauses should
be added.' One of them is found in the Tenth Amendment, which declares
that ' the powers not delegated to the United States by the Constitution, nor
prohibited by it to the States, are reserved to the States respectively, or to
the people.' The framers of the Constitution, as I have said, were
profoundly impressed with the evils which had resulted from the vicious
legislation of the States making notes a legal tender, and they determined
that such a power should not exist any longer. They therefore prohibited
the States from exercising it, and they refused to grant it to the new
government which they created. Of what purpose is it then to refer to the
exercise of the power by the absolute or the limited governments of Europe,
or by the States previous to our Constitution. Congress can exercise no
power by virtue of any supposed inherent sovereignty in the general
government. * * * There is no such thing as a power of inherent
sovereignty in the government of the United States. It is a government
of delegated powers, supreme within its prescribed sphere, but powerless
outside of it. In this country sovereignty resides in the people, and
Congress can exercise no power which they have not, by their Constitution,
intrusted to it; all else is withheld. It seems, however, to be supposed
that, as the power was taken from the States, it could not have been

intended that it should disappear entirely, and therefore it must in some way adhere to the general government, notwithstanding the Tenth Amendment and the nature of the Constitution. The doctrine, that a power not expressly forbidden may be exercised, would, as I have observed, change the character of our government. If I have read the Constitution aright, if there is any weight to be given to the uniform teachings of our great jurists and of commentators previous to the late civil war, the true doctrine is the very opposite of this. If the power is not in terms granted, and is not necessary and proper for the exercise of a power which is thus granted. it does not exist."

The uncertainty and confusion too often attending constitutional construction, as already shown, clearly demonstrate the wisdom of our fathers in insisting that religious liberty, freedom of speech and of the press, the right of the people peaceably to assemble and petition the government for a redress of grievances, of trial by jury in civil cases, that excessive bail should not be required, nor excessive fines imposed, nor cruel and unusual punishments inflicted, together with other important rights,—should be *expressly* guaranteed to the people as they are in the first ten amendments to the federal constitution, and that they should not be left to any mere implication.

When Rhode Island adopted the constitution eight states had ratified the first ten amendments. religious liberty. so far as the United States were concerned, being guaranteed in the first amendment. Rhode Island was the ninth state to ratify those amendments, but it was known when she took action, that the requisite number of states to make them operative would be obtained. When, therefore, Rhode Island's attitude towards soul-liberty is taken into consideration, is there not good ground to question whether the little commonwealth. after all. could have consistently ratified the constitution earlier than she did ?